12

Motivating the Disaffected

The ABC Approach to Classroom Behaviour Management

Steve Freer

The ABC Approach to Classroom Behaviour Management

Published by Lifetime Careers Wiltshire, 7 Ascot Court, White Horse Business Park, Trowbridge BA14 0XA.

ISBN 1 902876 68 7

Printed by Cromwell Press, Trowbridge
Cover illustration by Russell Cobb
Text design by Ministry of Design

Motivating the Disaffected
Series editor: Dr Gerald Lombard

The ABC Approach to Classroom Behaviour Management is one of a series of six titles designed to help professionals in education and advisory work to motivate and encourage students who are disengaged from learning.

Each book provides a concise and practical guide to topics that are of particular concern to teachers and advisers.

The other titles in the series are:

Asperger Syndrome and high functioning autism:
        guidelines for education post 16
Motivational Triggers
Social Competency: reading other people
Complex Specific Learning Difficulties
Staying Safe

To order copies, please contact Orca Book Services Ltd, Stanley House, 3 Fleets Lane, Poole, Dorset BH15 3AJ. Tel: 01202 665432. Fax: 01202 666219.

For further information about these and other products published by Lifetime Careers Publishing, please contact our customer services, tel: 01225 716023; email: sales@lifetime-publishing.co.uk, or www.lifetime-publishing.co.uk

Steve Freer

Steve is an Educational Consultant, helping schools and colleges address behavioural issues with challenging and vulnerable young people. He was a headteacher for 12 years in Dudley, West Midlands in a school for students with moderate learning difficulties and has 25 years' experience working with a range of young people with emotional and behavioural problems.

In one of his projects, he managed North Wiltshire's Young Peoples' Support Service to secondary schools, and helped to deliver a range of innovative and engaging approaches to re-motivate young people in schools.

Contents

Introduction

The aim of this publication is to offer the reader an initial framework and set of guidelines for successful classroom behaviour management.

It is called *The ABC of Classroom Behaviour Management* for two reasons. First, because it is drawn from theory and research around behaviour management and particularly with regard to the analysis of behaviour involving *Antecedents, Behaviours and Consequences.* The theory behind this *ABC* approach is that if problem behaviour occurs then it can be changed by altering the influences before the behaviour occurs (antecedents) or after it has occurred (consequences).

Secondly, it is the intention to give the reader '*A Basic Course*' or foundation for successful classroom behaviour management. The notion of ABC being at the very foundation of learning, in this case about classroom behaviour management, seemed eminently appropriate given the intention to provide readers with a good basis on which to build their knowledge and practice of classroom behaviour management.

Consideration will be given to the Antecedents, Behaviour and Consequences theory and analysis of behaviour in order to develop an understanding that behaviours can be changed by a careful and consistent management of conditions, environment and responses.

The publication will then go on to suggest how practitioners can use this theory in the classroom and offer four key areas as a straightforward and practical framework to help put theory into practice.

Section 1
The ABC of behaviour

The ABC analysis of behaviour makes it possible for us to look at behaviour and its causes, and as a result helps us work towards the shaping and managing of that behaviour. In the following pages we will give consideration to each component of the ABC.

Antecedents

Antecedents can be defined as those events or conditions within the environment that determine a particular behaviour or set of behaviours. If we are to successfully shape and manage behaviour then we must know about the environment in which that behaviour occurs. There are two key aspects of antecedents that we need to look at.

Settings

Settings are the stable, or relatively stable features of the environment in which behaviours occur. For example, the setting for sleeping is, generally, the bedroom. The classroom or workplace is usually the setting for attending to instruction and working. Being tired or unwell is often the setting in which a person shows irritable behaviours. Disrupted routines may be the setting in which some individuals become anxious.

Settings then, are the general context in which behaviours occur.

Triggers

Triggers are the signals that are present within the settings that 'set off' specific behaviours in a given situation. For example, the light being turned off in the bedroom is the trigger for children to close their eyes to go to sleep. The red traffic light acts as a trigger for drivers to apply their foot brakes. Triggers can either initiate behaviours or they can be the signal to stop ongoing activities. Triggers gain control over behaviours because they have been consistently associated with specific results during learning and inform the individual that a pleasant result is achievable or that an unpleasant result may be imminent.

Even within the context of this very brief outline of antecedents it is possible to appreciate the significance of the careful and consistent management of those environmental conditions that have an influence on student behaviour. For the practitioner in the classroom this means that thoughtful management and careful consideration of issues such as seating arrangements, practical work and student groupings could have a significant effect on how students behave.

Behaviour

Behaviours can be roughly grouped into three categories for our purposes. There are those behaviours that are new skills and need to be learned, there are behaviours that are unacceptable and need to be reduced or eliminated, and there are existing behaviours and skills that need to be encouraged and developed.

Behaviours are effected by environmental variables and as we have seen are determined by the settings in which a person finds themselves and are 'set off' by specific triggers. Behaviours always achieve some kind of result for the individual.

Consequences

Most behaviour is selected by its consequences. We tend to repeat behaviours that get us what we want and refrain from repeating behaviours that lead to occurrences we want to avoid. Simplistically, we can conclude that consequences may be described as 'rewarding' or 'punishing'. Rewarding consequences, which we will call positive reinforcers, are events that we seek out or 'go for'. We will, on the other hand, try to avoid punishing consequences. There are also those events that effect us neither way and these are called neutral consequences.

Logically then, it is reasonable to conclude that behaviours that are followed by positive reinforcers are likely to increase in frequency. Behaviours followed by punishing consequences tend to decrease in frequency while neutral consequences will have no effect on behaviours.

The ABC approach to behaviour management suggests that infrequent but desired behaviours (for example, following teacher instructions, getting on with work quietly, raising a hand to get attention), are made more frequent by arranging positive reinforcers, such as teacher attention and approval, to follow their occurrence. Undesired behaviours may be decreased in frequency by ensuring that positive reinforcers do *not* follow their occurrence, i.e. a neutral consequence is arranged. It may be necessary, however, to sometimes follow undesired behaviours with punishers (for example, a reprimand) in an attempt to reduce the frequency of the behaviour rapidly.

So that, in essence, is the ABC approach. The assumption is that if problem behaviour occurs because of particular antecedents and/or consequences, changing those influences can change it. By systematic management and use of antecedents, we are more likely to create a situation and environment in which appropriate behaviours will occur, and then by using positive consequences to reinforce those behaviours they are more likely to occur over again. Conversely, the systematic management and use of antecedents decreases the likelihood of inappropriate or unwanted behaviours occurring. Ensuring that these inappropriate behaviours are not reinforced by positive consequences or that punishing consequences follows them determines that they are less likely to occur again.

Having understood the theory of the ABC approach, the problem faced by most practitioners is how to translate that theory into practice when faced with a group or class of students! To attempt to do an ABC analysis of the behaviour of each member of a whole class is both bewildering and impossible. It is also unnecessary!

On the following pages is set out a clear and succinct framework that attempts to take the principles of the ABC approach and apply them to the management of whole classes or groups and the individuals within them.

Section 2
The ABC framework

This section applies the key principles of the ABC approach of behaviour to the classroom situation. The intention is to give the reader a solid foundation on which to base their management of behaviour within the classroom. It is not claimed that this approach will be 100% successful, all day and every day. Neither is it claimed that it will be successful with those students displaying more extreme and challenging behaviour. However, without such an approach in place in the classroom the practitioner will make little or no impact on the behaviour of the students for whom they are responsible and as a consequence the opportunities for effective teaching and learning will be greatly reduced. With the elements of this approach firmly in place, the practitioner will have a procedural checklist to which they may make reference when later attempting to manage the behaviour of more challenging students. With the majority of students carefully and consistently managed, the more challenging behaviour of the minority of students becomes easier to identify, analyse and tackle.

Most practitioners in schools and colleges find themselves stretched to the limit these days and are adept at the 'multi-tasking' demanded by our current education system. Add into this dimension the fact that staff in the classroom are likely to be involved in over 1000 daily interactions. They are likely to be asked to deal with unpredictable and unfamiliar events, some of which often occur simultaneously and frequently result in them having to make important decisions quickly. In fact classroom management has been described as 'perhaps the most complex and least understood situation on the planet. Managing classroom behaviour is a bit like air traffic control' (Watkins, 1999). Within this situation the need for a framework that gives the practitioner some clear guidelines and structure upon which to base the complex issue of classroom behaviour management and lays the foundation of success is of paramount importance.

The framework

If one were to dissect and analyse a series of lessons given by different staff it would become apparent that there are a number of key areas that are common to all. We would observe that unless staff took time to carefully structure and manage these areas then their overall effectiveness as classroom behaviour managers would be severely impaired.

There is no great mystery or complexity around these areas. They can be summarised into four parts:

- coming into the lesson

- start of the lesson

- during the lesson

- end of the lesson.

Smith and Laslett (1993) summarised the areas into four rules of classroom management:

- get them in

- get on with it

- get on with them

- get them out.

Our framework attempts to expand on these four rules by reference to the ABC approach and the works of eminent behaviour managers such as Canter and Canter (1992) and Rogers (1995).

The framework then is concerned with four key areas that are the essence of the management task facing classroom practitioners.

The first key area, *entry strategies* is concerned with management issues around ensuring students enter the classroom successfully and that lessons start smoothly and promptly.

The second area, *start right* is concerned with creating the right context for learning and ensuring work is appropriate for students.

The third area, *maintaining the momentum* examines the development of rules, rewards and procedures within the classroom and the development of sound working relationships between staff and students.

The fourth area, *end games* looks at how sessions finish and how students can leave classrooms in a positive way.

Before we look at each key area in some detail, it is worth stressing one or two underlying principles of the framework in order to establish a working context for the reader.

We believe that all staff have the right to teach, just as all students have the right to learn, in an environment that allows them to do just that. It should be free from disruption, in an atmosphere in which students can experience success and so develop self-esteem. However, such an environment does not just happen on the first day of a term or year! Staff must expect to have to work hard spending the time creating the right atmosphere in their classrooms. Unfortunately students of the 21st century often do not come to our schools 'oven ready' to learn. Good order doesn't simply happen, staff have to work hard to achieve it by setting high standards, having high expectations and by applying rules firmly and fairly. We believe that all students, whatever their age or ability, need structure, routines and boundaries in order that they learn successfully and develop self-esteem.

Now let's look at the key areas of the framework that can lead to the establishment of that successful learning environment:

Key area one: entry strategies

In our experience many practitioners seem reluctant to spend valuable curriculum time in order to establish key routines with students at the beginning of the academic year or term. The pressures on staff to deliver the curriculum seem to have an overriding priority and staff understandably feel that this is their key task, the fundamental yardstick by which they will be held accountable. Yet our experience also tells us that investing time in establishing key routines early in the year, particularly with new classes or groups, mean that teaching time can be used more effectively later in the year and in fact the net loss of teaching time is actually less. So let us examine these routines and practices, the antecedents, that can establish a positive setting to a lesson.

Be at your classroom on time

Seems obvious doesn't it? However, how many staff get to the lesson before the students, so they can prevent the pushing and barging in queues, so they can step in and nip in the bud the arguments and disagreements brought in from the playground? If we are concerned about managing antecedents and settings then here is a crucial yet simple way of doing so.

Meet and greet

Having arrived at the lesson punctually, here is the first opportunity for staff to set the tone of the lesson before students even enter the room. This is an opportunity to positively reinforce those behaviours you expect to see on a regular basis and the chance to reinforce your expectations to the group. It is also the chance to welcome students to the lesson in a positive, warm and up-beat manner. Make them feel that you really enjoy teaching them and that there is a great lesson ahead.

Decide how students are going to enter the room

A lot will depend on the age and maturity of students but staff will need to make it clear whether their students queue or congregate outside a room and wait for a signal before entering or whether they go straight into a room to meet staff. Either way it is essential to establish clear routines to settle students and to show a preparedness for lessons. Consider setting students a target time in which they should be seated, with outdoor clothes removed and with books/planners/materials ready. Take every opportunity to verbally positively reinforce behaviours you want to increase. Staff should devote their energies to positive reinforcement and not to highlighting students' behaviours that are inappropriate.

Do you need a seating plan?

Students should always enter the room in an orderly manner and where a student sits is to be decided by *staff*. Decisions about seating can have a significant impact on the triggers that set off particular student behaviours and so careful consideration should be given to the position and groupings of students. Having made the decisions staff should consider recording seating positions in some way so future disputes are avoided. If students change seats unofficially then there should be clear consequences to this behaviour.

Equipment and resource preparation

Having successfully managed students into the classroom many staff then lose the momentum they have gained by not giving adequate thought to the preparation and distribution of lesson materials and resources. Wherever possible staff should distribute resources prior to their students arrival, but should nevertheless always have a quick and efficient method of distribution worked out in advance. Staff should ensure that resources and materials are easily accessible to students and that potentially disruptive behaviour resulting from, for example, something as simple as a student not having the correct writing equipment, is quickly nipped in the bud by the establishment of quick and easy routines.

Key area two: start right

It has been made clear that careful and consistent management of the situation prior to a lesson is of critical importance to the success of the ABC approach to classroom management. We have seen that staff have opportunities to manage the antecedents and triggers to potential disruptive behaviour as well as having numerous opportunities to positively reinforce desired behaviours.

Key area two of the framework is concerned with the management of the environment within the classroom at the very start of lessons and we shall again see that opportunities are many and frequent for staff to set antecedents and to positively reinforce behaviours they want to increase.

Quiet start

It is of fundamental importance that staff only start lessons when all students are quiet and paying attention. In this way staff can at least be 100% sure that students have actually heard what is expected of them during the lesson. All too frequently we see staff in classrooms trying to talk over students that are talking when they are and then having to spend valuable time later in the lesson explaining expectations to students who either have not heard instructions or who have not been paying attention. In this scenario staff find it difficult to develop the management techniques that allow them to positively reinforce appropriate behaviours and to give their attention to students who are on task and following instructions. Without a quiet start it also means that staff will find it very difficult to implement effectively the remaining key areas of the framework.

Make learning aims clear

Do this at the start of the lesson, taking opportunities to link the lesson with previous learning experiences so students can immediately see both the purpose and context of the lesson. This gives students a clear focus to the lesson and immediately sets up expectations, potential achievement and success. Always write up as well as verbalise the aims of the lesson and in this way students can see and hear the 'big picture'.

Watch your language

Staff should always make sure that their language is clear and concise. Long and complicated sentences and instructions will only be followed by the most attentive and able students and the majority of the class will be left feeling unclear about what is expected. Short, clear and concise instructions given in a clear assertive tone will aid student understanding and aid effective learning. Lots of clear direction both later and throughout the lesson will help keep students on task.

Check understanding and expectations

Staff shouldn't suppose that because they have said it once everybody has immediately grasped the instruction! The use of open-ended questions to check that students have understood instructions is a useful technique. Asking specific students to explain what is expected reinforces and generalises everyone's understanding.

Step by step

Having made the learning aims clear to students the next step is to establish a similar clarity with regard to the structure of the lesson. Staff should make a point of explaining what is going to happen in the next 45 minutes to an hour, going through activities and tasks putting them into the context of the learning aims. Again tasks and activities should be written up and clearly displayed enabling students to both see and hear the plan. Such a strategy is particularly beneficial for students diagnosed with ADHD (Attention Deficit Hyperactivity Disorder) or Asperger Syndrome for whom change is often a problem, as it flags up that there will be a variety of activities and tasks throughout the lesson. However, the strategy is of benefit to all students because unexpected change in a lesson can cause untold disruption in a classroom and here is a method of managing the antecedents to potential inappropriate behaviour. An added advantage of making tasks and activities in the lesson very clear is that it is a perfect counter to the accusations from students that 'this is boring'. Staff are able to point out that although this bit may be boring, there is another more interesting activity coming up in a minute after they complete the current one. It's a bit like being told to eat your greens then you can have the ice cream!

Consider learning styles

Not all students can cope with a whole lesson of written work, so staff should always plan and organise lessons to keep students interested and so minimise the opportunities for disruption. Staff should try to build in opportunities for oral work and group work as well as for quiet individual work, thus catering for the varied learning styles of students. Give consideration to quizzes, games, computer work and different ways of presenting in order to make learning interesting and fun. One of the key reasons for disruptive behaviour in the classroom is that there is often a mis-match between students' ability and the work they are being asked to do. All practitioners should ensure that this trigger for disruptive behaviour is carefully managed and that differentiated learning opportunities are available for less-able students, thus allowing them to experience success and so build self-esteem.

Have high expectations

Having high, but realistic expectations of a group of students can be a corner stone of success and a key to self-esteem. Explaining learning aims and lesson tasks and activities should go hand in hand with challenge and expectation of students. Allied with staff enthusiasm for a subject area this challenge and expectation can be a big motivating factor for students. However, high expectations should reach beyond the academic domain and extend equally to student behaviour. Staff should expect students to always follow their directions and routines. They should remind their groups of expectations, rules and boundaries. The signalling by staff of positive expectations of behaviour is of fundamental importance. This is discussed in more detail in key area three.

It is worth emphasising at this point that the use of positive reinforcement is fundamental to the success of the ABC approach to classroom behaviour management. Remember we talked earlier about consequences and the fact that behaviours that are followed by positive reinforcers are more likely to increase in frequency. A basic positive reinforcer always available to staff is verbal praise and the attention that affords a student or students. Praise is the most meaningful, effective positive reinforcement you can give, and as Canter and Canter (1992) suggest, 'you can praise a student any time, any where'. Effective praise must always be genuine, so staff should avoid trotting out mouthfuls of superlatives such as 'well done', 'great' and 'fantastic' just as a matter of course. It soon becomes meaningless to students. Staff should use praise when they mean it, in other words it should be warranted. For praise to be used most effectively it should always be specific. When staff praise a student or students, they should make it clear why they are doing so. In other words they should highlight the behaviour that they are targeting. Finally, to use praise effectively staff should make it personal to an individual or group of students. The following sentence is an example of how to use praise effectively. 'Amanda and Jimmy, I really like the way you have both walked into the classroom and sat down quietly. Thank you.' It is genuine, warranted, specific and personal. It positively reinforces an appropriate behaviour in a public way, so reminding other students what is expected of them.

The careful management of antecedents through the establishment of clear, consistent routines and thorough planning and organisation of lessons is at the heart of the ABC approach to classroom management. The effective use of praise as a positive reinforcer is another of the essential elements of the approach. We will see in the next key area that staff can now build on these fundamentals by developing rules, routines and rewards, so that a rapport and relationship can develop with their students. In this way staff can continue to develop the confidence to effectively manage the class throughout the lesson.

Key area three: maintaining the momentum

Clear positive rules

We cannot expect students to behave in an appropriate way unless they are very clear about what we expect of them. Staff would be well advised to spend time not only agreeing the rules with students but also teaching them and frequently re-visiting them. In this way students are continually reminded of what is expected. We have already asserted that all students need structure, rules and boundaries, and well-written rules to help to define clearly those boundaries. Rules should be clearly displayed in the classrooms, visible to all students, and should be referred to frequently by staff. There are a few conventions worth noting regarding the establishment of rules.

- Choose classroom rules that let students know what behaviours are expected at all times. For example 'keep your hands to yourself'; 'always listen to staff'.

- Choose a limited number of rules (usually approximately five or six).

- Choose rules that are observable. Rules should address behaviours that staff can easily see. Vague rules are open to interpretation and cannot be readily reinforced. For example 'be in your seat when the bell rings' is far more specific and observable and less vague than, 'no messing around'.

- Choose rules that can apply at all times in the day. They should apply no matter what activity is taking place otherwise students will become confused and the ability of staff to teach students appropriate behaviour will be compromised.

- Choose rules that apply to behaviour only. Rules that cover, for example, homework create problems because there may be times when students do not understand work or when the completion of work is beyond their control.

It may well be that staff will want to involve students in the selection of rules in order to give them more ownership of what goes on in the classroom, thus increasing their motivation and the likelihood of success. Whatever rules are selected and by whatever method always remember, unless you know how you want your students to behave, how will they know?!

Clear set of rewards

We made the point earlier that many students today do not come to education 'oven ready' to learn. Staff must come to classrooms not only prepared to teach the subject matter, but to motivate students to behave appropriately as well. We have also endeavoured to make it clear that effective use of praise is one of the most powerful ways of positively reinforcing appropriate behaviours. Canter and Canter (1992) note that 'the single most important attribute we've found that distinguishes successful classroom managers from less effective ones is that they praise their students frequently'. So therefore, praise should be staff number one choice for positively recognising student behaviour.

Just as rules should be clearly displayed, so then should rewards for students so they are as equally clear about what is in it for them. Rewards as a way of positively reinforcing appropriate behaviours, can be loosely grouped into four areas.

Non-verbal

- Body language, for example, something as simple as a smile to give positive reinforcement of work or behaviour, but equally a thumbs up sign, a discrete pat on the back or similar can be very effective.

Verbal

- Verbal praise/approval/recognition – we all benefit from praise. Verbal feedback to all students in lessons is motivating. Remember to use personalised positive comments as described earlier.

- Telephone calls home to praise students.

- Praise and reward students by naming their behaviour back to them.

Written

- Positive written comments in books/folders, etc – use students' forenames.

- Letters of praise sent home. Postcards home saying how well students have worked.

- Certificates from subject areas.

- A subject book in which positive comments can be written.

- The use of praise slips.

- Stamps, commendations/merits, certificates of merit. These might well link to a school-wide hierarchy of rewards.

- Prizes for receiving a certain number of awards, for example vouchers, music, etc.

Public recognition

- Praise assemblies/good news sessions – please note that some students dislike public recognition and this sort of reward may not have the desired effect.

- Recognition via local media/school newsletter.

- Specific privileges, for example, use of facilities in school, an activity session or a social event.

- Increased responsibility.

- Headteacher/head of year awards.

There are, of course, a whole variety of ways in which students can be rewarded and their behaviour positively reinforced. The key is that they are clear about the system and that they understand it. Staff should not forget though that *regular consistent verbal feedback and praise* is at the heart of positive reinforcement.

Clear procedures

Ensuring that students know the classroom procedures will not only save staff valuable time but also help to avoid unnecessary disruption to the lesson. For example, it should be made clear that there is no shouting out and that in order to gain the attention of staff, students should signal in some agreed way. These things may be covered by class rules, but if not they will need to be taught to students. Staff will need to ensure that their students know the procedure to leave the room and that routine comments such as 'stop, pens down, look this way' or 'stop, look, listen' are well established and followed by all. Ensure that students are clear about procedures during practical sessions and that they know key safety routines. Again positive reinforcement by the effective use of praise should be the first strategy for staff rather than focusing attention on students who are not following procedures. Staff should always ensure that inappropriate behaviour is given a neutral consequence and that appropriate behaviour is always given a rewarding consequence.

Catch them doing something right

By now readers should be left in no doubt that the success of the ABC approach to classroom management is routed in the use of positive reinforcement, and in the effective use of praise in particular. To catch students doing something right is the essence of what we are advocating. To catch students following rules and showing appropriate behaviour, then to tell them and acknowledge the fact is an extremely powerful classroom management tool. The focus should be on appropriate behaviour, and when used spontaneously this strategy is very effective. For example, instead of breathing a sigh of relief when the class is quiet and working well, staff should take the opportunity to tell the group that they are doing well and recognise their achievement. A word of warning though, be careful that students are not embarrassed if praised publicly on an individual basis. A quiet word may be far more effective.

Praise systematically

We have seen that to use praise effectively it should be genuine, warranted, specific and personal. However, it should also be systematic and consistent. Staff should avoid a situation where praise is used regularly on a Monday morning and then not again until Wednesday afternoon! Research tells us that for praise to be really effective and have a real impact it should be used in a ratio of 4:1. So for every one negative comment staff should be using four positive or praise comments.

Be aware of yourself

Staff often lose sight of the significant impact they can have on student attitude and behaviour. The demeanour and persona of staff can colour student perception of a subject area and as a result have either a positive or negative effect on an individual's behaviour. It is critical that staff are aware of how they communicate with students both verbally and non-verbally. Staff want success for their students and few want to intimidate them, turn them off, leave them unmotivated or lower their self-esteem. However, even the best-intentioned teacher sometimes responds to students in ways that sabotage classroom management efforts. As Canter and Canter (1992) state 'it is your response style that sets the tone of your classroom'.

We can identify three general types of response style, two of which are reactive in style, i.e. they simply react to student disruptive behaviour, and one which is more effective and is proactive in nature where staff have positive expectations of their ability and plan accordingly.

Response style one: indecisive

This style is characterised by staff passiveness to student behaviour. Expectations are never clearly communicated and firm leadership is not given. Staff simply react to disruptive behaviour as it appears and as a consequence feel as though they are constantly 'fire fighting'. Response to inappropriate behaviour will be inconsistent, with a tendency to react to behaviour one day but ignore the same behaviour the next.

Indecisive staff are often heard using phrases such as:

'How many times do I have to tell you?'

'What am I going to do with you?'

'If you do that again you will be in detention for the rest of term!'

The body language of indecisive staff is characterised by poor eye contact, shrugs of the shoulders, a keeping of distance and a slumped body position.

As a result of this response style appropriate behaviour tends to get ignored, students are confused as to what is expected and often gain attention through inappropriate behaviour.

Response style two: overly authoritarian/aggressive

This style is characterised by rigid, authoritarian, 'iron fisted' discipline. There is a tendency to always tell students what to do, more often than not in an angry tone of voice. Staff responding this way use discipline to control students rather than to teach them how to behave in a positive manner. They tend to blame students, parents and senior managers for their problems. Staff responding in this style may well be able to get their needs met in the classroom but it is often at the expense of student feelings, dignity and self-esteem.

Overly authoritarian staff are often heard using a lot of sarcasm in the classroom, putting students down by phrases such as:

> *'It's about time you people did something you were told to do.'*

> *'That's it, I've had it with you. You've got a really poor attitude – one more word and you're out.'*

Overly authoritarian staff tend to shout a lot and are seen to get cross and lose their temper. Their body language is characterised by pointing and finger stabbing, glaring, leaning forward, an invasion of personal space and a general physical dominance.

As a result of this response style students can become angry in return and this can often affect other students in the class. This style discourages a positive attitude to learning and appropriate behaviour often goes unnoticed and unrecognised.

Response style three: positive/effective

A positive/effective response style is one in which staff clearly, confidently and consistently state their expectations to students and are prepared to back up their words with actions. Students are left in no doubt as to what is acceptable and not acceptable and are clear as to what will happen if they choose to behave appropriately or inappropriately. Staff using this response style have positive expectations of their ability to motivate students and this is reflected in words and actions. They seek to win cooperation by offering students choices, rather than to demand compliance. Students are challenged, spoken to and assisted thus helping promote independence, self-motivation and self control. Positive, effective staff take a leadership role in the classroom. Their body language is characterised by confident eye contact, open handed gestures, proximity to students without an invasion of space and the ability to turn away from a student in order to signal the end of an intervention or compliance with an instruction. Their facial expressions often give messages of approval, confidence, humour and questioning. As a result of this response style students feel safe and secure, they see a fairness of approach and they know where they stand. They feel respected and opportunities for teaching and learning are maximised.

No one member of staff responds in one single style all the time and in all situations. On a good day when feeling confident, staff may respond in a more positive and effective way. However, on a not so good day staff may well find more indecisive or aggressive responses creeping into their interactions with students. If staff are aware of the differences between the styles then they are more likely to be able to change into a positive and effective style when they find themselves responding indecisively or aggressively.

Develop classroom craft

It is essential that staff have impact and presence in the classroom. Having clear rules, rewards and procedures will give staff the confidence to develop and use a positive and effective response style, all of which will contribute to staff impact and presence. However, there are a few techniques that staff can use to develop their classroom behaviour management skills and so enhance their impact and presence. It is of crucial importance that staff move around the whole area of the classroom. They should be aware of blind spots and of inappropriate activity behind their backs. It is worth trying to always face the majority of the class most of the time. Managing by walking around gives staff opportunity to quickly defuse potential disruption merely by their close proximity to students, as well as the chance to quietly praise students verbally or non verbally or by written comments on their work. Developing the ability to scan is a worthwhile skill for staff to develop. This technique is useful when staff are working with a small group, while the rest of the class is working independently. If staff look up every few minutes and scan the class then take the time to notice and positively reinforce the students who are on task, then the likelihood of students continuing to work independently is increased.

When your momentum is disturbed

Despite all the careful and consistent management of antecedents and the consistent and effective use of praise and positive reinforcement staff will still be faced with situations in lessons that threaten to disrupt the learning of others and wreck the best laid lesson plans. A few techniques to redirect students displaying off-task behaviour are worth noting.

- Refer students who are off-task to class rules or code of behaviour and ensure that they know the consequences of their actions. This ensures a consistent approach.

- Maintain firm eye contact with students while discussing the problem behaviour. Always speak in a calm but firm way.

- Try the use of non-verbal signals, such as a raised eyebrow, or a shake of the head to let students know you are aware of their off-task behaviour. This is useful if you don't want to interrupt the flow of your input to other students.

- Use the look – stop what you are doing, look at the student, say nothing then continue with what you are doing.

- Stand by students who are off-task or behaving poorly. Ask whether they need help. If they do not then quietly restate your direction or expectation, i.e. 'I need/expect you to …'.

- Use the broken record technique, repeating the same point to the student despite his or her comments.

- When behaviour is a problem, staff should always speak calmly and quietly to the student. Make sure that you are not aggressive, but assertive and positive in your response. Ensure your actions are fair, just and consistent.

- Try to always avoid confrontation by ensuring that students are not backed into corners and that they have a clear choice to follow. In this way students will always have a way out. The message from staff to a student should be 'modify your behaviour or this will be the consequence'.

- Staff should focus on the deed and not the person. The message to students should be that it is their behaviour that is causing a problem, not them personally.

- Should staff need to reprimand the student it is often best done in private or at least quietly so as students can maintain their dignity.

We have learnt so far that clear routines, rules and procedures are significant contributors to the management of antecedents in our ABC approach to classroom behaviour management. They help to shape and create a learning environment where appropriate behaviours are more likely to occur. By establishing a clear set of rewards and applying them in a consistent way we are then able to positively reinforce appropriate behaviour in a systematic and effective way, thus significantly increasing the likelihood that they will be repeated. We have seen that the response style of staff and the development of a classroom craft can significantly enhance the relationship between staff and students and impact positively upon the implementation of the ABC approach in the classroom. In our final key area of the framework we look at the often forgotten end of the lesson and the advantages to staff and students of finishing off in the right way.

Key area four: end games

Our last key area deals with final stages of the lesson and looks at ways in which staff can ensure that their lessons are brought to a logical, timely and positive end rather than a rush and panic when the bell sounds. It is a short key area but nevertheless a crucial one.

Recap the aims of the lesson

This is a golden opportunity for staff to place in students' minds the degree of success and achievement attained during the lesson. Let all students know what they have learnt by summarising and recapping the tasks and activities that have resulted in a positive learning experience. This is again the opportunity to contextualise learning and allow students to see the link between lessons. If possible try and give an overview of the content of the next lesson and establish the link to future learning. This motivates students and sets up positive expectations and allows staff the opportunity to start managing the antecedents of appropriate behaviour for the next lesson!

Set homework

If it is appropriate to set homework staff should ensure this is done well before the end of the lesson. It is important that homework is written down and that staff check thoroughly that students have understood what is expected of them. Careful thought should be given to the quantity and degree of difficulty of homework, bearing in mind that some students may need support to complete work successfully.

Allow time to tidy away

Obvious but not always done! A significant amount of inappropriate behaviour occurs at the end of lessons when students are under pressure from harassed staff who have another group waiting outside in the corridor! Only instruct students to pack away when you are ready and ensure that materials, text books, etc are collected in and that students desks and area around them are tidy. If we are serious about managing antecedents and reducing triggers to inappropriate behaviour, then simple things such as allowing sufficient time to tidy away are crucial, not only to the class that are leaving but also to the class that are about to come in.

Give positive feedback

Staff should make sure that quality time is identified at the end of the lesson in order that they can give both class and individual rewards and feedback. This is a great opportunity to reinforce positively appropriate behaviours and let the class know how well they have done. Rewards that form part of a whole school system or even those that are just class-based can be issued or recapped and recorded. Staff should make every effort to refer to class routines, rules and procedures when giving reinforcement, feedback and rewards.

Dismiss positively

Just as staff are encouraged to 'meet and greet' in our first key area of 'entry strategies', so the same principles apply when dismissing students at the end of the lesson. Here is the opportunity to thank the class for their work and to bid them a friendly farewell. Make them feel that you have enjoyed teaching them and that you are looking forward to a productive and positive lesson next time. This approach builds self-esteem and helps develop a positive self-image among students and motivates students to your lesson and subject.

Manage the exit

It is most important that staff be in control during the dismissal procedure. The class you are just finishing with will be starting with a colleague in a few minutes and so you need to ensure that they leave you in an orderly and controlled manner, in the best possible frame of mind for the next lesson. Equally, staff need to make sure that they are giving the right signals and messages to the group waiting outside, by ensuring that their current group is dismissed in a calm and orderly way with the minimum of inappropriate behaviour. Staff should consider whether they require students to stand behind chairs before being dismissed or whether they need students to get bags, coats and equipment together prior to dismissal. For an orderly and controlled exit students will need to go a few at a time. Do not allow students to go before you give permission.

Section 3
Consequences: further considerations

We have now examined the four key areas of the ABC approach to classroom behaviour management and have offered the classroom practitioner a positive framework within which to work and operate in the classroom.

In the earlier explanation of the ABC of behaviour, reference was made to punishing consequences, i.e. those actions which, when applied directly after an inappropriate behaviour, tend to rapidly decrease the frequency of the behaviour. As has been made clear, the ABC approach to classroom behaviour management places its major emphasis on positive reinforcement within a carefully managed and structured framework of rules and procedures. If staff work hard at establishing the four key areas and are prepared to spend time developing not only the ABC approach but also their response style and their classroom craft then they should not have to revert to the use of punishing consequences more than occasionally.

However, as this approach is about clarity and as we have talked throughout about making explicit to students the consequences of appropriate and inappropriate behaviour, we need to spend some time looking at punishing consequences, or sanctions as we shall call them, in order to present a balanced approach to the use of consequences.

It has been quite deliberate not to include a discussion about the use of sanctions within the four key areas because to do so might have detracted from the central and key message about the powerful nature of positive reinforcement and the effective use of praise.

There is a need for a healthy balance between the number of rewards and sanctions available within the classroom and as we have already stated, research tells us that rewards should be applied in a ratio of 4:1 to sanctions. It is common sense to acknowledge that there will be times when students will choose not to follow the rules of the classroom. However, by careful planning, effective sanctions, and by working out in advance what will be the reaction, staff will have a course of action to follow and will avoid a reactive knee-jerk response.

Careful thought should be given to the choice of sanctions to be used. They must be something that students do not like, but never of course, anything that is either physically or psychologically harmful. Examples of sanctions that have operated effectively in schools include: being the last out of the class, missing free time, staying after lesson for one minute, time out and having parents contacted.

If sanctions are to be effective, and by that we mean that they are a helpful tool in teaching students how to behave appropriately, then it is essential that they be presented to students as a choice. It is in these circumstances that responsibility for a behaviour rests firmly with the students and you the practitioner are not seen to be victimising or 'picking on' anyone. Staff thus send a powerful message to the rest of the group that sanctions are actions that students know will happen when they choose to behave in an inappropriate way. It is essential that sanctions be seen as natural outcomes of inappropriate behaviours. Presenting a sanction as a choice to a student might go something like this:

> 'Josh, our rule is to allow others to work. If you pinch people's equipment you will choose to sit by yourself.'

(Josh's behaviour continues to be inappropriate.)

> 'Josh, you pinched Kate's pen. You have chosen to sit by yourself.'

Consistency and follow up are key here. By making sure that an appropriate sanction always follows an inappropriate behaviour, i.e. the breaking of a class rule, staff make a link for students between how they choose to behave and the outcome of behaviour.

Sanctions do not have to be severe to be effective. Many staff believe that the harsher the sanction the more effective it is. This is not the case and in fact the majority of students in a group will never go beyond a simple warning. For sanctions to be effective the key issue is not the degree of severity but rather the degree of consistency. It is the inevitability of the sanction that makes it effective. It is important therefore, that the sanctions chosen should be simple for staff to use in order that they can be applied in a consistent way. In our experience short 'time-wasting' sanctions are more effective than longer or more complex and severe ones.

Sanctions should be used in some kind of hierarchy and should always follow, and not precede, the strategies that staff would use to defuse, prevent or anticipate inappropriate behaviours. Some of these we have discussed in key area three of the framework. We would also expect staff to be using positive reinforcements to recognise the appropriate behaviours that were occurring in the group. Given that staff were adhering to the two points outlined above and a student was still behaving in an inappropriate way, then most staff would, as a first step, issue that student with a warning. This is a useful step because the student now knows that the next disruption will bring a 'real' sanction. If the disruption continues then staff need to use a sanction, such as a one-minute wait after the lesson has ended, sitting away from friends, brief time-out, etc. Staff should have clearly worked out a hierarchy of sanctions that they could use should the student choose to continue disruptive and inappropriate behaviour. Persistent and/or severe disruptive and inappropriate behaviour will more often than not result in the student being told to leave the classroom and in such cases the involvement of senior staff becomes inevitable. Staff should ensure that under this rare circumstance they are able to meet with the student and senior manager in order to emphasise that certain behaviours are totally beyond limits and to negotiate with the student the conditions under which they would be allowed back to the classroom. Finally, we need to consider some key points around the implementation of sanctions.

- Staff should provide sanctions in a calm, matter of fact manner. Always try to stay calm. Getting angry and shouting and demeaning students is counterproductive because it results in loss of dignity for both student and staff. Staff should point out to the disruptive students what they *should* be doing and *why* the sanction is being given.

- Be consistent. We have already discussed that it is the inevitability of the sanction and not the severity that guarantees its effectiveness. Staff should ensure that they provide a consequence every time a student chooses to disrupt.

- After a sanction, look to praise. There is a real temptation for staff to focus on negative behaviour after a sanction has been given to a student. Staff should always take the first opportunity to recognise and praise the student's appropriate behaviour after a sanction.

At this point our discussion about sanctions ends. However, it is well worth reiterating that the central philosophy of the ABC approach to classroom behaviour management is that the consistent use of positive reinforcement, particularly praise, in a structured and carefully managed environment will bring about an increase in appropriate behaviours and a decrease in inappropriate ones. Staff should ensure that they place their emphasis on the nature and use of the positive rather than on the use of the negative, in the form of sanctions. Although sanctions undoubtedly have a place, they should *never* be a first resort and indeed no resort at all until all other reasonable avenues have been pursued.

Conclusion

The aim of this publication has been to give staff who work in the field of education a basic foundation upon which they can build an effective way of managing classroom behaviour. This has been done by offering a framework that is based around four key areas and an attempt to demonstrate the link between the theory of behavioural analysis and the practice of behaviour management.

Practical and real scenarios of classroom management have been offered in the hope that practitioners will find the framework relevant, easy to understand and not too difficult to implement. Tips and guidelines have been based upon many years of 'front-line' experience as well as a knowledge and healthy respect for theory and research in the field of behaviour management.

The material that has been presented here is the start of an on-going process and certainly not the final word. It was acknowledged earlier that classroom management was an extremely complex issue. It is the author's fervent hope that staff will take the framework and develop it by using the skills and techniques suggested and adapting them to their own personal teaching style and to the unique needs of their students. Staff may want to integrate some of the concepts found here with other theories and approaches to managing student behaviour. In short, it is hoped that staff will take the framework and build upon it. What else is a foundation for?

References

Canter, L. & Canter, M. (1992), *Assertive Discipline: Positive Behaviour Management for Today's Classroom*, Santa Monica, USA: Lee Canter & Associates.

Rogers, B. (1995), *Behaviour Management: A Whole School Approach*, Scholastic Australia.

Smith, C. J. & Laslett, R. (1993), *Effective Classroom Management: A Teacher's Guide*, (2nd ed), London: Routledge.

Watkins, C. (1999), *Managing Classroom Behaviour – Research to Diagnosis*, London: Institute of Education University of London/ATL.